Why can't I...
live underwater
with the fish?

and other questions
about water

Distributed in the United States by
Smart Apple Media
2140 Howard Drive West
North Mankato, Minnesota 56003

Editor: Claire Edwards
Designer: Jacqueline Palmer
Picture researcher: Diana Morris
Consultant: Anne Goldsworthy

The Library of Congress has cataloged the hardcover edition as follows:

Hewitt, Sally.
    Live underwater with the fish? / written by Sally Hewitt.
        p. cm. — (Why can't I)
    Includes index.
    ISBN 1-930643-00-4 (hardcover)
    ISBN 1-59389-079-6 (pbk.)
        1. Water — Miscellanea — Juvenile literature. [1. Water — Miscellanea.
    2. Questions and answers.] I. Title. II. Series.

    GB662.3 .H478 2001
    553.7 — dc21

                                                    2001027182

Printed in China

9 8 7 6 5 4 3 2 1

Picture acknowledgements:
Peter Cade/Stone: front cover montage br, 3c, 23br. Ron Dahlquist/Stone: 24b background.
Tim Davis/Stone: 9b. Patricia Doyle/Stone: 8bl. Hackenburg/Powerstock-Zefa: 21tc, 26tr.
Michael Keller/Stockmarket: 16cr. Klaus Lahnstein/Stone: 21t background. Sally Morgan/
Ecoscene: 14b. Roy Morsch/Zefa-Stockmarket: 25c. Claire Paxton: 24trc. Pictor International:
10-11 background. Powerstock-Zefa: 5 background. John M Roberts/Stockmarket: 20 background.
Steve Satuchek/Image Bank: 14-15, 15tr. Ariel Skelley/Stockmarket: 18c. Stuart Westmorland/
Stone: front cover montage bl, 22bl, 27br. Art Wolfe/Stone: 3t & b, 22b, 23cr.
Norbert Wu/Stockmarket: front cover background, 22-23.

All other photography by Ray Moller.

Why can't I...

live underwater
with the fish?

and other questions
about water

Sally Hewitt

Chrysalis Education

Contents

Why can't I hold water?

Because water is liquid.

It doesn't have a shape that you can hold.

It flows and spreads out everywhere, unless it is in a container.

Why can't I pour ice?

Because ice is solid water.

When liquid water is very cold, it freezes into a lump. The name for solid water is ice.

You can't pour solid things like ice, a brick, or a cake.

Try it and see!

Why can't I stand on a cloud?

Because a cloud is like mist floating high in the air.

Mist is really lots and lots of tiny bits of water and ice.

If you tried to
stand on a cloud
you would fall
straight through.

9

Why don't marbles float?

Because marbles are heavy for their size.

The marbles push down
on the water as they sink.
At the same time,
the water pushes them up.

The marbles are small,
but they are too heavy
for the water to hold up,
so they sink.

Why won't a balloon sink?

Because a balloon is light for its size.

It is big and full of air, but it isn't heavy.

The water pushes against it and holds it up in the water.

Why can't I walk on water?

Because you are much too heavy for the water to hold up.

Some very light insects can walk on water.

The top of the water is like a very thin, stretchy skin. The insects are so light they don't break it.

Why can't I find a raindrop in a river?

Because raindrops mix with the river water.

A raindrop has a kind of stretchy skin. This holds the water in a round shape as it falls through the air.

When the raindrop splashes down, the skin breaks.

Why can't I pour water upward?

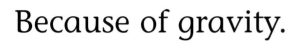

Because of gravity.

Gravity is a force that pulls
everything on Earth down
toward the ground—
even water.

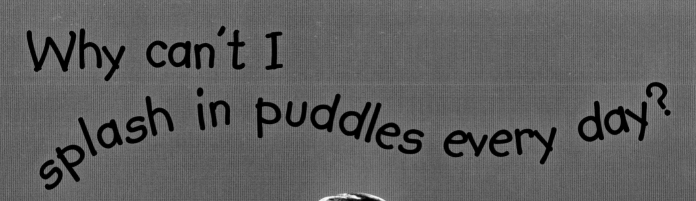

Why can't I splash in puddles every day?

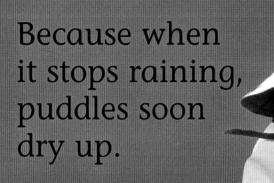

Because when it stops raining, puddles soon dry up.

The water becomes tiny drops in the air too small for you to see.

Why won't my sweater keep me dry in the rain?

Because your sweater soaks up the rain and makes you wet.

To keep dry, you need to wear waterproof clothes that don't soak up water.

Why can't I see dew all day?

You only see dew
when the air is cool.

Dew is made of tiny drops of water.
As the air warms up in the sun,
the water goes into the air.

Why can't I keep my snowman until summer?

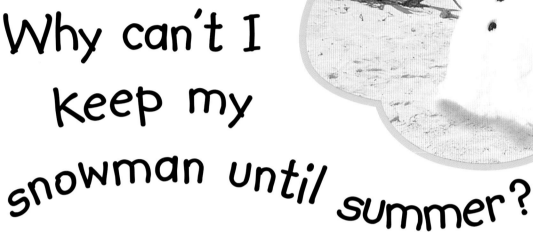

Because snow melts
in warm weather.

Snow is made up of icy snowflakes
that fall from clouds on a winter day.

When the air warms up, the snow
melts and changes back into water.

Why can't I live underwater with the fish?

Because you need to breathe air.

You breathe the air all around you in and out of your lungs.

Fish can live underwater because they take in air mixed in the water. They use special flaps called gills.

Why can't I drink seawater?

Because seawater is salty
and tastes horrible.

The water you drink isn't salty.
It comes from rainwater,
or rivers and lakes.

Why can't I live without water?

All living things need water to live and grow.

Your body is mostly water, and you need to drink plenty of water to keep healthy.

Watery words

cloud Tiny drops of water and bits of ice in the sky.

dew Drops of water that appear in the cold night air.

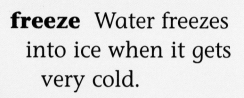 **freeze** Water freezes into ice when it gets very cold.

gas Air is made of gas, and so is water vapor. Usually we can't see it. Gas does not have a shape of its own.

ice Water that has frozen solid.

liquid Something that doesn't have a shape of its own and that we can pour. Water is a liquid.

Here are some places you find water:

sea, river, lake, puddle, waterfall, fountain, faucet

Can you draw them all? Can you think of some of the things you use water for?

24

melt Ice and snow melt into water when they become too warm to stay frozen.

rain Drops of water that fall when they become too big and heavy to stay up in the clouds.

sea Oceans of salty water that we can't drink.

snow Flakes of frozen water that fall to the ground.

solid Something that has a shape of its own. Ice is solid water.

A mix-up

Can you put the words below into groups with these headings: **Snow, Rain, Mist, Ice,** and **Pouring Water**. Some words may belong in more than one group.

slush

drip

drop

iceberg

splash

monsoon

fog

hail

dew

sleet

wet

smog

Can you write a poem using some of these words?

drizzle

moist

icicle

cascade

frost

cloud

overflow

downpour

bubble

snowflake

gurgle

damp

spray

pour

Notes for parents and teachers

The answer to the question "Why can't I stand on a cloud?" might be obvious to an adult, but it probably isn't to a child. Before reading the simple, factual answers that follow the questions in this book, spend time together exploring the exciting possibilities that the questions raise. Use your imagination and enter a world where the impossible becomes possible.

Back to reality!

Floating and sinking

Collect all kinds of objects of different sizes, shapes, and made of different materials—such as coins, balls, a cork, a sponge, and a pencil. Guess which will float and which will sink. Put them in water and discuss what happens. Group the objects into those that float and those that sink.

Take two similar-sized pieces of aluminum foil. Leave one piece of foil flat. Fold the other piece in half, pressing down firmly. Fold it in half again. Keep folding it until you have a very small piece of flat foil. Try floating both pieces of foil. What happens now?

28

Melting and freezing

Pour water into different-shaped containers—
for example, a yogurt container and a mold
for sand play—and freeze them. Tip the ice
shapes onto a tray and watch them melt back
into water at room temperature. Talk about
ice being frozen water, and compare solid ice
with melting ice and liquid water.

Fill a glass with ice cubes. Ask your child to
guess how much water will be in the glass
when the ice cubes melt. Talk about what
actually happens.

Pouring and flowing

Collect plastic containers, including empty
plastic bottles, squeezey bottles, plastic
pitchers, and yogurt containers. The more
varied the shapes and sizes, the better. Play
together with the containers in a bowl of
water or in the tub. Pour water from one to
the other. Ask questions such as: Which do
you think holds the most water? Can you
pour water faster from the squeezey bottle
or the pitcher?

Evaporation

Draw a chalk line around a puddle after a
rain shower. Check the size of the puddle once
an hour. Does it stay the same size? Discuss
what happens to the water.

Hang some wet clothes out to dry. Discuss
what happens to the water. Notice how long
the clothes take to dry in different weather.

Index